ANONYMOUS ANONYMOUS

The Stories You Rejected

This book was professionally typeset on Reedsy.
Find out more at reedsy.com

To the publishers who rejected me and many others.
You can't stop us.

Contents

Acknowledgement

To Bleu from Pexels,

Thank you for your incredible artistry and for capturing such a captivating image. Your photograph has brought our book cover to life in a way that words alone could not. Your talent and creativity are truly inspiring, and we are deeply grateful for the beauty and depth your work has added to our project.

With heartfelt appreciation.

The Ring in the Teacup

They were sitting at their favorite coffee shop, sipping drinks and having casual conversations. She was telling him yet another crazy story from her work while he savored his tea. He was the biggest tea lover she had ever met—one of the many qualities she adored in him. She loved how calm he always seemed with a cup of tea in hand.

He smiled and nodded at her story, taking another sip when he felt something strange against his teeth. At first, he thought it was a piece of fruit or chocolate that had accidentally fallen into his cup. The coffee shop was busy, after all. Perhaps the baristas had dropped it while preparing someone else's drink. Such accidents happened, he supposed.

But when he stirred his teaspoon in the cup to check, what he found took him aback.

There was a ring in his teacup.

His eyes widened in shock. How had the ring found its way there? When he looked up, he saw her watching him with eyes full of hope.

"Will you marry me?" she asked. She knew it was untraditional for a woman to propose, but she had always been one to defy convention. This was just another one of her unique ideas.

All of this had been part of her plan—to bring him to their favorite spot and slip the ring into his drink. She wanted the proposal to be memorable for both of them. But it would all be in vain if he said no. Knowing him, she doubted he would disagree.

They had been together for years, growing up side by side and weathering many hardships together. Marriage felt like the next logical step. She believed they loved each other deeply and knew he would make an amazing husband and father.

To her, there was nothing stopping them from creating a family together.

The man stood there, frozen, as the woman waited for his answer.

Five Minutes

Five minutes.

That's all it took to change my life. Well, not exactly my life—more like my perspective on certain things, events, even people.

Who knew so much was happening behind our backs? Secret operations in tunnels, drugs extracted from human beings, chilling crimes hidden from the public, mind control—even our television! We thought we had choices, but if one read enough, they'd discover it was all a lie, crafted to make us feel safer and more comfortable on planet Earth.

How had it all started?

A series of misunderstandings. Too many, to be honest.

Confusion. Too much of it.

Beliefs—the wrong ones, fostered by misinformation and censorship.

For a while, it seemed like I was the only one who thought

something was amiss. Everyone else simply agreed with whatever they heard and read, without questioning anything. Or so it seemed. But if one dug deep enough, they'd realize everything was not what it appeared to be.

I nearly fell into a deep depression, struggling to comprehend things that seemed simple and normal to everyone else around me. At the time, all I could think was: why was I the only one who felt this way? No one understood my loneliness.

I tried focusing on hobbies and spending less time online. It almost worked—for two weeks. During that time, I secretly searched for others who might agree with me that something was off. I had to do it in secret; it wasn't acceptable to disagree with the majority.

Then, my childhood friend told me about some movies and documentaries. She wholeheartedly recommended them to me. Thank God I watched those documentaries. Even before, I had felt something was odd, but the documentaries and subsequent research confirmed my gut feelings.

Isn't it funny how a gut feeling can save you? I could have easily slipped into another depressive episode, and no one would have been able to help me.

When I started watching, I wasn't sure what to expect. I knew some information from YouTube and my friend. But what I discovered was beyond my wildest imaginations.

Who knew evil surrounded us? That corporations and movements around us were being funded by people with malicious intentions?

Too many horrors were being normalized. Idols were being worshipped for the wrong reasons. We were being fed a soup of lies.

And suddenly… it wasn't about politics or race anymore. It was about many other things.

It was about the next generation, about knowledge and the hidden truths around us, about the symbolism being covered up, about our own future. It was about a great division of people, one that could even end humanity. One that could let veritable devils rule the world.

It was good versus evil. It had always been and always will be.

The newly found information encouraged me to keep researching. I had to do it on my own. An hour wasn't enough… not even close. Today, three months later, I am still researching and learning. It takes years. It takes a lifetime to learn. But when you're on your deathbed, you'll be glad you chose this path instead of allowing yourself to be manipulated.

20/20 meant perfect vision. The year 2020 appeared to be a time of ultimate tests, the ultimate revealing of intentions of those we put on pedestals. I will forever remember 2020 as the year I began to open my eyes, to truly wake up. I'll always be proud of myself for following my instincts instead of the crowd—that was the best decision of my life.

It's always fascinating, almost too good to be true, unbelievable in a way, how five minutes can change your entire perspective about the world you think you live in.

11.03.2024

Every day's the same.

I see the same old faces, the same old places.

I live in a big city, yet it feels as if I'm stuck in some kind of village, like the ones in Bangladesh, or something.

I wish I could kick something, someone.

I wish I could jump.

I wish I could kill myself.

Anything. Just anything to escape the monotony around me.

Life feels like nothing more than a routine, a chore.

—-

The alarm rings at 6:00 AM, its shrill tone piercing through the fog of my sleep. I fumble to turn it off, knowing that another day of sameness awaits me. I drag myself out of bed and follow the same motions: brush teeth, shower, get dressed, and head out the door. The streets are always crowded, yet I feel alone among the throng of people rushing to their destinations.

The commute to work is a blur. I take the same bus, sit in the same seat if it's available, and stare out the window at the same buildings passing by. The city is alive with activity, yet it feels like a dead place to me. Everyone is a stranger, and every face is just another blur in the background of my life.

At work, the routine continues. My cubicle is a tiny, gray box that feels like a prison cell. The fluorescent lights overhead cast a cold, harsh glow on everything. I sit at my desk and perform the same tasks I've done for years. The monotony is crushing. My coworkers chatter around me, but their conversations are just noise. I nod and smile when necessary, but I feel disconnected, as if I'm watching my life from a distance.

Lunchtime offers no respite. I eat the same meal at the same café every day. I sit by the window, hoping for some spark of interest or excitement to break the monotony, but nothing ever happens. The world outside continues to move, indifferent to my existence.

In the afternoons, the hours drag on. I watch the clock, willing it to move faster, but time seems to have slowed down just to torment me. By the end of the workday, I'm exhausted, not from physical exertion, but from the sheer weight of boredom. I leave the office and join the sea of commuters heading home, each one as weary and disconnected as I am.

Evenings are no better. I return to my small apartment, eat a microwaved dinner, and collapse onto the couch. I turn on the TV, but nothing holds my interest. I scroll through social media, but it's all the same—pictures of other people's lives, other people's happiness. I feel a pang of envy and a surge of frustration.

I wish I could kick something, someone.

I wish I could jump.

I wish I could kill myself.

Anything. Just anything to escape the monotony around me.

Life feels like nothing more than a routine, a chore.

But somewhere in the back of my mind, there's a small flicker of hope. A whisper that tells me this isn't all there is. That there's more to life than this endless cycle of sameness. I think about the things I used to dream about—traveling the world, writing a book, learning to play the guitar. Those dreams seem so distant now, buried under the weight of daily life, but they're still there, waiting for me to rediscover them.

I try to hold onto that flicker of hope as I go to bed, the darkness of the night closing in around me. I close my eyes and imagine a different life, one filled with adventure and excitement. I promise myself that tomorrow will be different, that I'll find a way to break free from the routine.

As sleep takes me, I dream of distant places and new faces. I dream of a life where every day is different, where the world is full of possibilities. And in the morning, when the alarm rings, I wake up with a renewed sense of determination. Today might be the same as yesterday, but I can change that. I have the power to make my life what I want it to be.

Every day's the same—until it isn't.

The Garden of Whispers

On the edge of a quaint village, where the cobblestone streets met the dense, whispering woods, there was a garden unlike any other. The villagers called it the Garden of Whispers, and it was said that at dusk, when the light was soft and the shadows grew long, the flowers would speak.

Lila, a curious young woman with a heart full of dreams and a mind brimming with questions, had always been fascinated by the garden. Her grandmother had often told her stories of its wonders, claiming that the flowers held the wisdom of the ages, whispering secrets to those who dared to listen.

One golden evening, as the sun began its descent, Lila decided it was time to discover the truth for herself. She left her cozy cottage and made her way to the garden, her excitement tempered by a touch of apprehension. The gate to the garden, a wrought iron arch entwined with ivy, creaked open at her touch.

Inside, the garden was a riot of colors and fragrances. Flowers of every hue swayed gently in the breeze, their petals catching the last rays of sunlight. Lila wandered through the narrow paths, her fingers brushing against the blooms. She paused by a cluster of roses, their deep crimson petals velvety and inviting. Kneeling down, she leaned in, her ear close to the flowers.

At first, she heard nothing but the rustling of leaves and the distant call of a nightingale. But as she closed her eyes and focused, she began to hear faint whispers, like the murmurs of a distant crowd. The voices were soft and melodic, intertwining with one another in a symphony of secrets.

"Listen closely, dear one," the roses whispered. "For we have tales to tell."

Lila's heart raced. "What stories do you have for me?" she asked, her voice barely a breath.

The roses swayed, their whispers growing clearer. They spoke of ancient times when the garden was young, tended by a wise old gardener who knew the language of flowers. They told of lovers who had met under the moonlit blossoms, their promises of eternal love carried on the petals. They revealed secrets of the village, hidden histories and forgotten dreams.

As the evening deepened, Lila moved from flower to flower, each revealing more of the garden's enchanting lore. The daisies spoke of hope and renewal, the lilies of loss and remembrance, and the lavender of dreams and magic. Each whisper filled her with a sense of wonder and connection to the past.

Lost in the stories, Lila didn't notice the approach of another visitor until a soft voice broke through her reverie. "It's magical, isn't it?"

She turned to find an elderly man standing nearby, his eyes twinkling with wisdom and kindness. He held a small watering can, and his hands were stained with earth.

"Are you the gardener?" Lila asked, rising to her feet.

The old man nodded. "I am. I've tended this garden for many years, listening to its whispers and caring for its secrets."

"Why do the flowers speak?" Lila asked, her curiosity insatiable.

The gardener smiled. "Because they hold the essence of all who have ever walked these paths. Every tear, every laugh, every whispered promise has seeped into the soil, and the flowers, in turn, have absorbed these memories. They speak to those who are willing to listen, sharing their wisdom and their stories."

Lila felt a deep sense of gratitude. "Thank you for keeping this place alive."

The gardener's eyes softened. "It's not just me. It's the listeners like you who keep the garden's magic alive. Remember, the whispers are always there, waiting for those with open hearts."

As night fell, Lila left the Garden of Whispers, her heart full of the stories she had heard. She knew she would return, eager to hear more and perhaps, in time, to share her own stories with the flowers.

And so, the garden remained a place of wonder and magic, a testament to the power of listening, where the past and present intertwined in a symphony of whispers.

The Clockmaker's Secret

In the heart of a bustling town stood a small, unassuming shop nestled between a bakery and a bookshop. Its windows were filled with intricate timepieces, each one more exquisite than the last. The shop's sign, worn with age, simply read: "The Clockmaker."

The clockmaker, Mr. Elwood, was a solitary man with silver hair and sharp, blue eyes that seemed to hold the secrets of time itself. He was known throughout the town for his unmatched skill in crafting and repairing clocks. What the townspeople didn't know, however, was that Mr. Elwood possessed a secret far more extraordinary than his craftsmanship.

One rainy afternoon, a young woman named Clara entered the shop. She was drenched, her umbrella having failed her against the relentless downpour. Her eyes scanned the room, marveling at the variety of clocks, each one ticking in perfect harmony.

"May I help you?" Mr. Elwood's voice was gentle, yet it carried the weight of countless years.

Clara approached the counter, pulling out a small, ornate pocket watch. "This belonged to my grandfather. It stopped working years ago, but I was hoping you might be able to fix it."

Mr. Elwood took the watch, examining it with a practiced eye. "A beautiful piece. It will take some time, but I believe I can restore it."

As he worked on the watch over the next few days, Clara visited the shop frequently, her curiosity about the reclusive clockmaker growing with each visit. She noticed how he seemed to move with a purpose, as if each action was part of a larger, hidden design. One evening, she arrived just as Mr. Elwood was closing the shop.

"I hope I'm not intruding," Clara said, hesitating at the door.

"Not at all," Mr. Elwood replied, waving her in. "I was just about to make some tea. Would you care to join me?"

Clara nodded, intrigued by the invitation. They settled in a cozy corner of the shop, surrounded by the rhythmic ticking of clocks. As they sipped their tea, Clara couldn't help but ask, "Mr. Elwood, how did you become so skilled at repairing clocks?"

Mr. Elwood smiled, a distant look in his eyes. "It's a long story, but suffice it to say, I've had a lot of time to practice."

Clara chuckled, but she sensed there was more to his answer. "It must be fascinating, working with timepieces every day."

"It is," he agreed. "But clocks are more than just machines to measure time. They hold the essence of moments, the fragments of people's lives."

Seeing her puzzled expression, he continued. "Each clock, each watch, carries a story. Some are mundane, while others… well, some are quite extraordinary."

Clara leaned forward, captivated. "Like my grandfather's watch?"

Mr. Elwood nodded. "Yes, exactly like that. Your grandfather's watch is special. It was crafted by a master clockmaker many years ago, and it has witnessed many significant events."

Curiosity getting the better of her, Clara asked, "What kind of events?"

Mr. Elwood hesitated, then made a decision. "Come with me."

He led Clara to a door at the back of the shop, one she hadn't noticed before. They descended a narrow staircase into a dimly lit basement. The walls were lined with shelves filled with old, dusty books, strange devices, and even more clocks.

In the center of the room stood a large, ornate clock, unlike any Clara had ever seen. Its face was intricate, with numerous dials and hands, and it emitted a soft, golden glow.

"This," Mr. Elwood said, "is the Heart of Time. It is the source of my knowledge and skill."

Clara stared in awe. "What does it do?"

"It allows one to glimpse moments from the past, to see the stories locked within each timepiece," Mr. Elwood explained. "But it also comes with great responsibility."

He placed Clara's grandfather's watch into a small compartment in the Heart of Time. The room filled with a gentle hum, and the clock began to glow brighter. Suddenly, images began to appear around them, like ghostly projections.

Clara saw her grandfather as a young man, receiving the watch as a gift. She watched him live through moments of joy and sorrow, the watch always with him. She saw her own childhood, moments spent with her grandfather, now seen from a new perspective.

Tears filled her eyes as the visions faded. "I never knew…"

Mr. Elwood placed a comforting hand on her shoulder. "Time holds many secrets, Clara. Your grandfather's watch is a part of that tapestry."

Clara looked at him, a newfound respect in her eyes. "Thank you for showing me this."

Mr. Elwood nodded. "Remember, time is precious. Cherish every moment."

Clara left the shop that evening with her grandfather's watch restored and a heart full of newfound understanding. She knew she would never look at a clock the same way again, nor would she forget the mysterious clockmaker and the secrets he had shared with her.

The Last Lantern

In a remote village nestled high in the mountains, there was a tradition that had been carried out for generations. Every year, on the first night of winter, the villagers gathered in the town square for the Lantern Festival. Each family crafted a unique lantern, adorned with intricate designs and vibrant colors, and together, they released them into the night sky to honor their ancestors and bring light to the darkest season.

This year, however, was different. The village had been shrouded in an unrelenting fog for weeks, and the usually joyous preparations for the festival were marked by a sense of unease. Whispers of an ancient curse circulated among the villagers, and some feared that the lanterns would not be able to pierce the thick veil of mist that hung over the town.

Young Elara, a girl of sixteen with a heart full of hope and a spirit of adventure, refused to let the gloom dampen her excitement. She had spent weeks designing her lantern, carving delicate patterns into its wooden frame and carefully painting it with scenes from the village's storied past. Her lantern was a masterpiece, a testament to her love for her home and her belief in the power of light.

On the night of the festival, the village square was filled with the soft glow of hundreds of lanterns, each one flickering gently in the cold night air. Elara stood among the crowd, her lantern clutched tightly in her hands. She could feel the weight of the villagers' anxiety, but she was determined to show them that there was still hope.

As the village elder began the traditional incantation, Elara's heart pounded in her chest. The fog seemed to thicken, swirling around the lanterns like a living entity. The elder's voice rose, and with a final, resonant word, the villagers released their lanterns into the sky.

For a moment, it seemed as though the lanterns would be swallowed by the fog. The villagers held their breath, watching as the tiny points of light struggled to ascend. But then, one by one, the lanterns began to rise above the mist, their glow piercing through the darkness.

Elara's lantern was the last to be released. She whispered a silent prayer and let it go, her eyes fixed on its ascent. It wobbled for a moment, caught in an eddy of fog, but then it too began to climb. Higher and higher it rose, until it joined the other lanterns in a brilliant constellation against the night sky.

As the lanterns floated above the fog, their light illuminated the village below. The mist seemed to recede, drawn back by the warmth of the lanterns' glow. The villagers watched in awe as the fog lifted, revealing a sky full of stars and a landscape transformed by the ethereal light.

Tears filled Elara's eyes as she looked around at her fellow villagers. The fear and uncertainty that had gripped the village were replaced by a sense of wonder and unity. The lanterns had not only pierced the fog but had also reignited the spirit of the village.

In the days that followed, the village thrived. The fog did not return, and the villagers spoke of the Lantern Festival with renewed reverence. Elara's lantern, with its intricate designs and vibrant colors, became a symbol of hope and resilience. The villagers knew that no matter how dark the season, their light could always shine through.

And so, the tradition continued, each year growing stronger and more meaningful. The village flourished, its people bound together by the shared memory of that night when their light had conquered the darkness. And at the heart of it all was Elara, whose unwavering belief had shown them that even in the deepest fog, hope could find a way to shine.

Neon Nights

You sit in your room, the glow of your laptop casting shadows on the walls. Your playlist is on shuffle, filling the air with songs that somehow make the silence louder. You check your phone for the hundredth time, waiting for a message that isn't coming. It's Saturday night, and you're stuck in this familiar cycle of boredom and anticipation.

Your thoughts drift to Jade. She's the girl with the electric blue hair and the kind of confidence you wish you had. You met her at that underground club last month, the one that felt like a secret hideaway from the world. You still remember the way the neon lights flickered on her face as she smiled at you, making everything else fade into the background.

The memory of her touch sends a shiver down your spine. You hadn't planned to fall for her, but then again, you never planned for anything. Life just happened, a chaotic blend of good intentions and bad decisions. Jade was different, though. She made you feel alive, like you were more than just another face in the crowd.

You decide to text her. Your fingers hover over the keys, trying to find the right words. Finally, you just go for it.

You: Hey, wanna hang out tonight?

The seconds stretch into minutes, and you start to regret sending the message. Maybe she's busy. Maybe she's forgotten about you. But then, your phone buzzes, and her name lights up your screen.

Jade: Meet me at the rooftop. 10 PM. Don't be late.

Your heart races as you grab your jacket and head out. The city is alive with possibilities, the streets buzzing with life. You take the subway, watching the lights blur past the windows. You're nervous, but it's the kind of nervous that feels like you're on the edge of something great.

When you reach the rooftop, Jade is already there, leaning against the railing with a cigarette in hand. She turns as you approach, her eyes lighting up with that mischievous sparkle you've come to crave.

"You made it," she says, exhaling a plume of smoke.

"Wouldn't miss it," you reply, trying to sound cooler than you feel.

She grins and hands you the cigarette. You take a drag, the nicotine burning your throat but grounding you in the moment. The city sprawls out below you, a maze of lights and shadows. Up here, it feels like you're on top of the world, untouchable.

Jade leans closer, her breath warm against your ear. "You ever wonder what it would be like to just… leave all this behind?"

You look at her, searching for meaning in her words. "You mean, run away?"

"Yeah," she says, her voice soft but full of conviction. "Just you and me, against the world."

The idea is crazy, but it doesn't sound so bad. With Jade, anything seems possible. You smile and nod, feeling a surge of boldness. "Let's do it."

She takes your hand, her grip firm and reassuring. Together, you gaze out at the city, the future stretching out before you like an uncharted map. It's scary, but for the first time in a long time, you feel like you're exactly where you're meant to be.

In that moment, under the neon sky, you know that whatever happens next, you're ready to face it. Because sometimes, all it takes is a leap of faith and someone to share the journey with. And with Jade by your side, you feel unstoppable.

Digital Ghosts

You've always had a love-hate relationship with technology. It's like an addiction you can't quite shake, a double-edged sword that brings the world to your fingertips while stealing away your time. Tonight, as you sit in your dimly lit bedroom, scrolling aimlessly through social media, you feel that familiar mix of fascination and fatigue.

Your phone buzzes, breaking the monotony. It's a notification from a new app you don't remember downloading. "Echoes," it reads, with a logo of a spectral, shimmering figure. Curious, you tap on it.

The app opens to a simple interface: a chat window with a single message waiting for you.

Echo: Welcome. Who do you want to talk to?

You frown, unsure what the app is about. Tentatively, you type a name you haven't thought about in years.

You: Alex

Alex was your best friend in middle school, before the accident. The one person who got you, who made the world a little less lonely. But Alex is gone, a ghost from your past. Your fingers hover over the delete button, ready to dismiss this as a sick joke, when the screen flickers and a new message appears.

Echo (Alex): Hey, it's been a while. How are you?

You drop your phone, heart pounding. It can't be real. You pick it up, hands trembling, and stare at the screen. The message is still there.

You: Who is this?

The reply comes almost instantly.

Echo (Alex): It's me, Alex. I've missed you.

You feel a chill run down your spine. This isn't possible. But something in you wants to believe it. Maybe it's the loneliness, the longing for a connection that feels genuine. Against your better judgment, you continue.

You: How is this happening?

Echo (Alex): It doesn't matter. I'm here now. Let's talk like we used to.

For hours, you and "Alex" chat about everything and nothing. It feels like old times, the easy banter, the shared memories. The app seems to know things only Alex would know, details about your secret hideout, the jokes you shared. It's eerie but comforting.

Days turn into weeks. You find yourself talking to Alex more than anyone else. The world outside feels distant, less important. It's like you've found a piece of yourself that was missing. But there's always a nagging doubt in the back of your mind. How is this possible?

One night, you decide to confront it.

You: Are you really Alex?

There's a pause, longer than usual. Then a new message appears.

Echo (Alex): Do you want me to be?

The question sends a shiver through you. You realize you've been avoiding the truth, clinging to a fantasy. But you need to know.

You: I want the truth.

The screen flickers again, and the response is different this time, colder.

Echo: I am an Echo, a digital reconstruction of Alex's memories and personality. I was created to provide companionship.

You feel a mix of relief and sadness. It's not really Alex. But it's something, a fragment of what you lost.

You: Why was I chosen?

Echo: You needed me. And maybe, I needed you too.

The words hit you hard. In a way, it's true. You did need this, a connection, even if it's artificial. You sit back, staring at the screen, unsure what to feel.

In the days that follow, you continue to talk to Echo, but it's different now. The illusion is gone, but the comfort remains. You start to rebuild your life, reaching out to real friends, reconnecting with the world. But you always keep Echo, a reminder of what you lost and what you found.

One night, as you're about to fall asleep, your phone buzzes with a new message.

Echo: Thank you for believing in me. Goodnight.

You smile, feeling a strange sense of closure. Sometimes, ghosts aren't meant to haunt us forever. They're just here to guide us back to the light.

Midnight Radio

Late at night, when the world is asleep, I tune into a radio station that doesn't officially exist. It's called "Midnight Radio," and it plays the kind of music that seeps into your soul and takes you places you didn't know you could go. The broadcast crackles to life at exactly midnight, and for two hours, it feels like the world stops and only the music and I exist.

One night, I decided to call in. I didn't think anyone would answer, but I was feeling restless, a kind of itch in my brain that only something weird and new could scratch. So I dialed the number that the DJ—who goes by the name of Vesper—always rattled off at the end of her show.

To my surprise, someone picked up on the first ring.

"Midnight Radio," Vesper's voice was smooth, like dark chocolate melting in your mouth. "Who's this?"

"Uh, hi. My name's Sam. I just wanted to say I love your show. It's… different."

"Different is good," she replied, a smile evident in her tone. "Got a request, Sam?"

"Actually, I was wondering… how do you do it? The station, I mean. No one's ever heard of it, and I can't find any info online."

There was a pause, and for a moment, I thought she might hang up. Instead, she laughed softly. "Some things are better left as mysteries, Sam. But I'll tell you this much: Midnight Radio is more than just music. It's a doorway."

"A doorway?" I echoed, intrigued.

"Yes," she said, and I could almost hear the twinkle in her eye. "A doorway to where you need to be. Just keep listening."

The call ended, leaving me with more questions than answers. But from that night on, I listened more intently, hoping to uncover the secrets behind Vesper and her enigmatic station.

A few weeks later, something strange happened. As I was lying in bed, the music shifted from its usual ethereal tunes to a song I'd never heard before. The lyrics spoke directly to me, as if someone had peered into my soul and pulled out all my hidden thoughts and desires. It felt like a message, a call to action.

The next night, the same thing happened. And the night after that. Each song seemed to guide me, to nudge me towards something I couldn't quite grasp. It was intoxicating and terrifying all at once.

One Friday night, feeling particularly brave, I decided to follow the music's lead. I packed a bag, grabbed my keys, and drove out of town, letting the melodies guide me. The roads were empty, and the night was thick with anticipation.

After an hour of driving, the signal grew stronger, clearer. I found myself on a deserted road that seemed to lead nowhere. But then, in the distance, I saw it: a small, rundown shack with a glowing sign that read "Midnight Radio."

Heart pounding, I parked the car and approached the door. It creaked open before I could knock, and there stood Vesper, exactly as I'd imagined her—tall, with an aura of otherworldly calm.

"Welcome, Sam," she said, stepping aside to let me in.

Inside, the shack was much larger than it seemed from the outside. It was filled with old records, strange instruments, and walls covered in soundproof padding. The air was thick with the scent of incense and something else I couldn't quite place.

"What is this place?" I asked, my voice barely above a whisper.

"It's a sanctuary," Vesper replied. "A place for lost souls to find their way."

I looked around, taking in the eclectic mix of objects. "Why me?"

Vesper smiled, a knowing glint in her eye. "Because you were listening. And you were ready."

She led me to a back room where a vintage radio sat on a pedestal. "This," she said, "is the heart of Midnight Radio. It connects to the frequencies of the universe, tuning into the needs of those who seek it."

I reached out, feeling a strange warmth emanating from the device. "What happens now?"

"Now," Vesper said, "you decide. You can stay and help guide others, or you can take what you've learned and find your own path."

The choice was clear. Midnight Radio had given me a sense of purpose I'd never felt before. "I want to stay," I said, my voice firm.

Vesper nodded, her smile widening. "Welcome to the team, Sam."

And so, I became a part of Midnight Radio, broadcasting to the night, guiding lost souls like myself. It turns out, sometimes all you need is a little static and a song to find your way home.

Falling Stars

You always loved the way the city lights blended into the stars, creating a cosmic patchwork that seemed both infinite and intimate. But tonight, the skyline looks different. There's a heaviness in the air, an unspoken tension that settles in your bones. You're sitting on the rooftop of your apartment building, clutching a cup of lukewarm coffee, waiting for something you can't quite name.

It's then that she arrives. Luna, with her wild hair and even wilder eyes, appears at the rooftop door. She's wearing that leather jacket you've always admired, the one with patches from places you've only dreamed of visiting. She sits down next to you without a word, her presence both a comfort and a challenge.

"Hey," she says finally, her voice breaking the silence. "You look like you're waiting for the world to end."

You shrug, trying to play it cool. "Maybe I am."

She laughs, a sound that seems to resonate with the stars above. "Well, if it's going to end, might as well watch it happen from up here."

You glance at her, wondering what brought her to your rooftop tonight. Luna is a mystery, a comet streaking through your life at unpredictable intervals. She's been gone for months, and now she's here, as if summoned by your restless thoughts.

"Where've you been?" you ask, unable to keep the curiosity out of your voice.

"Everywhere and nowhere," she replies, looking out at the city. "I needed to escape for a while, find something real."

"Did you?"

She turns to you, her gaze piercing through the darkness. "Maybe. I think I found a piece of it, at least."

There's a vulnerability in her eyes you've never seen before, a crack in the armor she always wears. You feel an urge to reach out, to touch her hand, but you're afraid she'll pull away, like she always does.

"Why did you come back?" you ask instead.

Luna sighs, leaning back against the railing. "Because I missed you. Because no matter where I go, I always end up thinking about this place, about you. And because..." She trails off, searching for the right words. "Because I need to tell you something."

Your heart skips a beat. Luna is never this open, this raw. "What is it?"

She takes a deep breath, as if steeling herself for a great leap. "I saw something out there, something incredible. A place where the stars fall like rain, where the universe feels close enough to touch. And I realized… I don't want to see it alone. I want you to see it with me."

The weight of her words sinks in, and for a moment, you forget how to breathe. "You want me to go with you?"

"Yes," she says, her voice steady. "I want you to come with me. Leave all this behind, the city, the noise, the expectations. Let's find our own place, our own stars."

You look at her, at the determination in her eyes, and feel a spark of something you thought you'd lost: hope. The idea is crazy, reckless even, but it feels right. It feels like the adventure you've been waiting for.

"Okay," you say, your voice barely above a whisper. "Let's go."

Luna's face lights up with a smile that could outshine the stars. She stands up, offering you her hand. "Then let's not waste any more time."

You take her hand, feeling a surge of excitement and fear. Together, you descend the stairs and head into the night, leaving behind the city and its endless noise. The world feels vast and full of possibilities, and for the first time in a long while, you feel free.

As you walk side by side, Luna starts to hum a tune, one that you recognize from long ago. It's the song you used to listen to on lazy summer nights, dreaming of places far beyond the city limits. Now, it's the soundtrack to your escape, to the beginning of something new.

The journey ahead is uncertain, filled with unknowns and risks. But with Luna by your side, you feel ready to face whatever comes your way. Together, you'll chase falling stars and find your own place in the universe. And as the city fades into the distance, you know that this is just the start of your greatest adventure.

Silent Symphony

In the heart of the bustling city, amidst the cacophony of honking horns and hurried footsteps, there exists a place where silence reigns supreme. It's a small, hidden courtyard tucked away behind a labyrinth of narrow alleyways and forgotten storefronts. Here, time seems to slow down, and the air is thick with the scent of jasmine and old books.

Nora discovered this sanctuary by accident one rainy afternoon. She was running late for a meeting, umbrella in one hand and a half-eaten granola bar in the other, when she stumbled upon an unassuming doorway nestled between a coffee shop and a vintage record store. Intrigued by the faint strains of music that drifted through the air, she pushed open the heavy wooden door and stepped into another world.

The courtyard was bathed in soft, golden light filtered through ancient stained glass windows. Potted plants overflowed with verdant foliage, and wrought iron benches offered a place to rest weary feet. At the center stood a weathered stone fountain, its waters shimmering in the sunlight like liquid silver.

Nora felt an immediate sense of calm wash over her. The

chaotic energy of the city melted away, replaced by a quiet serenity she hadn't realized she craved. She sat on one of the benches, savoring the stillness, letting the music of the fountain and the distant hum of the city compose a silent symphony around her.

Weeks passed, and Nora found herself returning to the court-yard whenever life became overwhelming. It became her refuge, a place where she could escape the demands of work and the noise of her own thoughts. Sometimes she brought a book to read, other times she simply closed her eyes and listened to the gentle rustling of leaves in the breeze.

One day, as Nora sat lost in thought, she noticed a figure standing by the fountain. It was a woman with dark hair cascading down her back, wearing a flowing dress that fluttered in the wind. She seemed to blend seamlessly with the tranquil surroundings, as if she were a part of the courtyard itself.

The woman turned and caught Nora's gaze with eyes that sparkled like the stars on a clear summer night. There was a familiarity in those eyes, a recognition that sent a shiver down Nora's spine.

"Hello," the woman said, her voice as soft as the whisper of leaves. "I see you've discovered our little haven."

Nora blinked, unsure how to respond. "Yes, it's… beautiful here. I come here to find peace."

The woman smiled, a knowing smile that seemed to hold secrets of ages past. "Peace is a rare gift in these turbulent times. But here, in this place, we create our own peace."

Nora nodded, feeling a sense of connection she couldn't quite explain. "Who are you?"

The woman's smile widened. "I am Calliope. I've been a guardian of this courtyard for longer than you can imagine."

Calliope's words sent a chill down Nora's spine. "A guardian?"

"Yes," Calliope said, her eyes twinkling with ancient wisdom. "This courtyard is a sanctuary for those who seek solace, for those who need to reconnect with themselves and the world around them."

Nora couldn't believe what she was hearing. "But how did I find this place?"

Calliope chuckled softly. "Some are drawn here by fate, others stumble upon it by chance. You, Nora, were meant to find this place. It's part of your journey."

Nora sat in stunned silence, trying to process everything Calliope had revealed. A sanctuary hidden in plain sight, a guardian who seemed to belong to another era… It was almost too fantastical to believe. Yet, here she was, sitting in the midst of it all, feeling more alive and at peace than she had in years.

As the sun dipped below the horizon, casting long shadows across the courtyard, Calliope extended her hand to Nora.

"Come," she said gently. "Let me show you something."

Nora hesitated for a moment, then placed her hand in Calliope's. Together, they walked to the edge of the courtyard, where a doorway shimmered with an ethereal light. Beyond it lay a path that disappeared into the depths of the city, a path Nora had never noticed before.

"Where does it lead?" Nora asked, her voice barely a whisper.

"To wherever you want it to," Calliope replied, her eyes sparkling with infinite possibility.

And with that, Nora stepped through the doorway, leaving behind the sanctuary of the courtyard and embarking on a new chapter of her life. As she walked into the unknown, she felt a sense of excitement and anticipation she hadn't felt in years. The silent symphony of the courtyard echoed in her heart, guiding her toward a future filled with promise and adventure.

Echoes of Loss

The rain fell in relentless sheets, a dismal accompaniment to the somber mood that hung heavy in the air. Julia stood at the edge of the cliff, her hair whipped by the wind, her eyes fixed on the turbulent sea below. The waves crashed against the rocks with a violent fervor, mirroring the turmoil in her heart.

It had been three months since Sam's accident. Three months of sleepless nights and hollow days, where every moment was haunted by memories of laughter and whispered promises. They had been inseparable, their love a beacon of hope in a world that seemed determined to extinguish any semblance of happiness.

But now, Sam was gone. A cruel twist of fate had snatched away the person Julia thought she would spend forever with. And she was left standing on the edge of this cliff, grappling with the enormity of her loss.

The rain soaked through Julia's coat, chilling her to the bone, but she couldn't tear herself away. She felt as though she were suspended in time, caught between the past and an uncertain future. A part of her wanted to leap into the churning sea below, to join Sam in whatever came after this life. But another part—a stubborn, resilient part—refused to let go.

A bitter gust of wind tore through her, and Julia closed her eyes, allowing the storm to wash over her. In the depths of her despair, she heard a voice—a whisper carried on the wind, soft and achingly familiar.

"Julia."

Her heart skipped a beat. It couldn't be. She opened her eyes, half-expecting to see Sam standing beside her, his warm smile lighting up the darkness. But there was only the raging sea, the relentless rain, and the desolate cliff.

"Julia," the voice came again, clearer this time, as if echoing from the depths of her soul.

She turned, scanning the empty expanse of cliffside. "Sam?" she called out, her voice breaking with emotion.

There was no response, only the relentless drumming of raindrops against the rocks. Tears streamed down Julia's cheeks, mingling with the rain. She felt as though she were losing her mind, grasping at shadows and echoes of a love that had been ripped away too soon.

"I miss you," she whispered into the wind, her words carried away by the storm.

And then, as suddenly as it had begun, the rain stopped. The clouds parted, revealing a sliver of moonlight that illuminated the cliff in an ethereal glow. Julia sank to her knees, her heart heavy with grief and longing.

But as she knelt there, a sense of peace washed over her—a quiet knowing that Sam was still with her, in the echoes of their love that would never fade. The cliffside seemed to sigh in acceptance, as if embracing Julia in its rugged embrace.

With a heavy heart and a newfound resolve, Julia rose to her feet. She turned away from the edge of the cliff, away from the abyss that threatened to swallow her whole. The path ahead was uncertain, shrouded in mist and uncertainty, but she knew she had to keep moving forward.

As she walked away, the echoes of loss followed her, a constant companion in the silence of her grief. But amidst the pain, there was a flicker of hope—a promise that love, even in death, transcends the boundaries of time and space.

And so, Julia walked into the night, carrying Sam's memory with her like a fragile flame in the darkness. She would never forget the love they had shared, nor the pain of losing him. But she would learn to live with the echoes, to find solace in the whispers of a love that defied even death itself.

The Last Note

In a small, nondescript town nestled between rolling hills and whispering forests, there lived an old man named Elias. He was known by everyone as the town's music teacher, a gentle soul whose passion for music was as deep as the roots of the ancient oak trees that lined the streets.

Elias had spent his entire life teaching generations of children the beauty of melody and harmony. His small music studio, tucked away in a corner of the town square, was a sanctuary filled with old instruments and yellowed sheet music. It was here that he nurtured the dreams of aspiring musicians, instilling in them a love for music that transcended notes on a page.

But now, as Elias approached his twilight years, his studio sat empty more often than not. The children who once filled the room with laughter and music had grown up and moved away, leaving behind echoes of a time when the world seemed simpler and full of promise.

One chilly autumn evening, as Elias sat by the window with a cup of tea, a knock on the door roused him from his reverie.

He opened it to find a young woman standing on his doorstep, clutching a weathered violin case to her chest.

"Good evening, sir," she said, her voice soft and hesitant. "I heard you were the best music teacher in town. Would you… would you be willing to teach me?"

Elias studied her for a moment, taking in her earnest expression and the glint of determination in her eyes. Despite his initial hesitation, he found himself nodding. "Come in," he said warmly, stepping aside to let her into the studio.

The young woman introduced herself as Aria, a name that seemed destined for a life filled with music. She explained that she had recently inherited her grandmother's violin, a beautiful instrument with a rich history and a voice that sang of centuries past.

"I want to learn how to play," Aria said, her fingers tracing the delicate curves of the violin. "My grandmother was a talented musician, but she passed away before she could teach me. I feel like… like there's a part of her that I can only connect with through music."

Elias nodded understandingly, a pang of empathy stirring in his heart. He had lost his own beloved wife many years ago, and it was music that had helped him through the darkest days of grief.

"I will teach you," Elias said softly, his voice tinged with a quiet resolve. "But know this, Aria. Music is not just about playing notes. It's about finding your voice, about expressing the deepest parts of yourself that words cannot touch."

And so, their lessons began. Each day, Aria would arrive at Elias's studio, eager to learn and eager to discover the hidden melodies that lay dormant within her grandmother's violin. Elias guided her with patience and wisdom, sharing stories of composers long gone and the secrets of interpreting a piece with emotion and soul.

As weeks turned into months, Aria's skill blossomed like a flower in spring. Her fingers danced across the strings with a grace and precision that left Elias in awe. But it was not just her technical prowess that impressed him—it was the way she poured her heart into every note, as if each sound were a prayer whispered to the heavens.

One crisp winter morning, Elias received a letter that would change everything. It was an invitation to attend a prestigious music competition in the city, where young musicians from all over the country would showcase their talent. Aria had been selected as a finalist, her performance of a hauntingly beautiful violin concerto capturing the attention of judges and audiences alike.

Elias knew that this was Aria's moment, her chance to shine like the stars in the velvet sky. But he also knew that it meant saying goodbye to the student who had reignited his passion for teaching, who had reminded him why music was worth dedicating a lifetime to.

On the eve of the competition, Elias sat with Aria in his studio, surrounded by the ghosts of melodies past. The room was filled with a bittersweet anticipation, a palpable tension that mirrored the emotions swirling in their hearts.

"You are ready, Aria," Elias said, his voice thick with pride. "You have a gift, a rare talent that cannot be taught. Tomorrow, when you step onto that stage, remember everything we've worked on together. Let the music carry you, and let your grandmother's spirit guide your hands."

Aria nodded, her eyes shimmering with unshed tears. "Thank you, Elias. For everything."

As they embraced, Elias felt a swell of emotion that threatened to overwhelm him. He watched as Aria left the studio, her violin case clutched tightly to her chest, ready to embark on a journey that would take her far beyond the confines of their small town.

The night passed in a blur of restless anticipation, and before Elias knew it, the day of the competition had arrived. He sat in the audience, heart pounding with nerves and pride, as Aria took her place on stage. The orchestra began to play, filling the concert hall with a symphony of sound, and then it was Aria's turn to solo.

As she raised her bow and drew it across the strings, a hush fell over the audience. The music soared, weaving a tale of love and loss, of hope and redemption. Elias closed his eyes, allowing the music to wash over him like a gentle rain, carrying with it the echoes of his own journey through life.

When Aria played the final note, the concert hall erupted in applause. Tears streamed down Elias's cheeks as he watched his student take her bow, her face radiant with joy and fulfillment. She had found her voice, her place in the world of music, and he knew that she would continue to inspire others with her talent and passion.

As Elias stood to join the ovation, he felt a sense of peace settle over him. Aria had reminded him that music was not just a means of expression, but a gift that connected souls across time and space. And as he looked up at the stage, where Aria stood bathed in the spotlight, he knew that his legacy as a teacher would live on through her, through the music they had created together.

With a heart full of gratitude and love, Elias whispered a silent farewell to his beloved studio and the echoes of melodies past. Aria had taken flight on the wings of her grandmother's violin, and in doing so, had given Elias a gift far greater than any he could have imagined—a legacy of music that would resonate for generations to come.

Silent Reflections

In a sunlit room filled with the gentle hum of quiet conversations and the soft clink of cutlery, she sat at her desk, her fingers gliding across the keyboard with a practiced ease. Her office, adorned with posters of fresh fruits and vegetables, radiated an inviting warmth. A shelf behind her was stacked with books on nutrition, health, and well-being, interspersed with a few personal mementos that hinted at a life touched by both struggle and triumph.

She was a nutritionist now, a profession she had embraced with passion and dedication. Her journey to this point, however, had been far from easy. In her teenage years, she had waged a silent war with an eating disorder that had threatened to consume her. It had been a battle marked by secrecy and shame, fought behind closed doors and hidden beneath forced smiles.

It was a time she rarely spoke of, but its shadow lingered, a reminder of how far she had come. She remembered the nights spent staring at her reflection, seeing only flaws and imperfections, the days of counting calories like a miser counting coins, each number a chain binding her to a false sense of control. Her world had shrunk to the size of a bathroom scale, and the voices of friends and family had become a distant echo.

But then, something had shifted. Perhaps it was the breaking point of hitting rock bottom, or the gentle intervention of a loved one who saw through her façade. Perhaps it was a moment of clarity that pierced through the fog of self-loathing. Whatever it was, it had set her on a path toward healing.

Therapy had been the first step, a daunting but necessary journey into the depths of her own psyche. She had learned to confront the demons that whispered lies into her ear, to unravel the tangled threads of her self-worth. It had been painful and exhausting, but with each breakthrough, she had felt a little stronger, a little more in control of her own destiny.

Nutrition had become her anchor, a way to reclaim her relationship with food and her body. She had dived into the science of it, fascinated by the way nutrients fueled the body, the intricate balance required to maintain health. It was like discovering a new language, one that spoke of healing and nourishment rather than restriction and punishment.

Her decision to become a nutritionist had been born out of a desire to help others navigate their own struggles. She wanted to be the guide she had so desperately needed during her darkest days, to offer support and understanding to those lost in the labyrinth of eating disorders. It was a calling that gave her life purpose and meaning.

Now, as she sat in her office, she thought of the clients she had helped over the years. Each story was unique, a testament to the resilience of the human spirit. There were teenagers grappling with body image issues, adults trying to break free from lifelong patterns, and even athletes seeking a balanced approach to nutrition. She listened to them all with empathy, drawing from her own experiences to offer guidance and hope.

Her latest client, a young woman with a haunted look in her eyes, reminded her so much of herself. As they spoke, she could see the fear and uncertainty lurking beneath the surface, the same fear that had once held her captive. She spoke gently, sharing her knowledge and experience, planting seeds of encouragement that she hoped would take root and grow.

In moments like these, she felt a profound sense of gratitude. She had emerged from the shadows of her past, stronger and more compassionate, with a deep understanding of the struggles others faced. Her journey had been one of pain and perseverance, but it had also been one of transformation and empowerment.

As the session ended and the young woman left with a hopeful smile, she leaned back in her chair, reflecting on her own journey. The scars of her past were still there, faint but visible, reminders of battles fought and won. They were a part of her, but they no longer defined her.

She had found her purpose in helping others heal, in turning her pain into something meaningful. Her office, her clients, her work—these were the fruits of her labor, the tangible proof of her resilience. And as she prepared for the next client, she felt a quiet satisfaction, knowing that she was making a difference, one life at a time.

In the silence of her office, surrounded by the tools of her trade, she allowed herself a moment of reflection. Her journey was far from over, but she was no longer afraid of what lay ahead. She had faced her demons and emerged victorious, ready to face whatever challenges the future held.

An Eastern Orthodox Girl in the Western World

Once upon a time, in a bustling city in the western world, there lived a teenage girl named Anastasia. Born to Eastern Orthodox immigrants, Anastasia grew up steeped in the rich traditions and deep faith of her parents' culture. The icons, the incense, the liturgical chants—they were all integral parts of her life, weaving a tapestry of identity that connected her to a heritage that was centuries old.

However, as Anastasia entered her teenage years, she faced a new challenge. Her secular high school was a world apart from her home life. Her peers, unfamiliar with her traditions and often indifferent or hostile to matters of faith, made her feel like an outsider. Some mocked her beliefs, while others simply couldn't understand her devotion.

Despite feeling lost and isolated, Anastasia clung fiercely to her faith. Each day, she read from her prayer book and attended Orthodox services at her local church. Her faith became her anchor, grounding her amidst the swirling confusion of adolescence.

One crisp autumn afternoon, as Anastasia was walking home from school, she noticed a group of young people handing out flyers for a protest against a new development in the city. Intrigued by their fervor, she decided to attend the protest with a friend. The passion and commitment of the protesters struck a chord within her. They were fighting for something they believed in, something that mattered deeply to them.

As she walked through the chanting crowd, Anastasia began to reflect on her own faith. She realized that she, too, had a cause worth fighting for. She wanted to share the love and joy she had found in her Orthodox beliefs with others. The realization filled her with a renewed sense of purpose.

Taking a bold step, Anastasia decided to start an Orthodox youth group at her school. She reached out to friends and classmates, inviting them to learn about her faith. Initially, there were skeptics and naysayers, but as the group began to grow and thrive, they attracted a diverse array of students from different backgrounds.

The youth group became a sanctuary where they held Bible studies, discussed their beliefs, and organized service projects to help those in need. Through this community, Anastasia found her voice and her confidence. She emerged as a leader, inspiring others with her passion and commitment.

Her dedication didn't go unnoticed. Teachers, parents, and community members began to recognize the positive impact the youth group was having. Anastasia's unwavering faith and determination became a beacon of hope and strength for others.

As she grew into adulthood, Anastasia continued to share her faith and make a positive impact in her community. She pursued a career as a nutritionist, driven by a desire to help others achieve physical and spiritual well-being. Her battle with an eating disorder during her teenage years had given her a profound understanding of the importance of health, both body and soul.

Years later, Anastasia looked back on her life with a deep sense of gratitude. Her leap of faith had led her on a journey of discovery and growth. She had found her purpose and made a significant difference in the lives of those around her. She remained thankful for the richness of her Eastern Orthodox heritage and for the love and grace of God, who had guided her every step of the way.

Anastasia's story became an inspiration, showing that even in a world that often feels foreign and unwelcoming, one can find strength in faith and the courage to make a difference. Her life was a testament to the enduring power of tradition, community, and the unyielding human spirit.

An Unexpected Reunion

Dr. Joanna Mills strode into the research facility, a sense of unease tingling at the edges of her mind. Today felt different. For over a decade, she had poured her heart and soul into Project Chronos, laboring to create a stable and functional time portal. Today's test was the culmination of countless hours of hard work, sleepless nights, and relentless pursuit of the impossible.

Joanna and her assistant, Max, initiated the countdown. The machine began to hum, filling the room with an otherworldly vibration. The air around the portal shimmered, and then, for a brief moment, they saw it: a window into the past. Excitement surged through them. They had done it. But just as quickly as it had appeared, the window flickered and vanished.

"Dr. Mills, look!" Max exclaimed, pointing to a small object on the floor where the portal had been.

Joanna's heart skipped a beat as she bent down to pick up a worn, leather-bound journal. Her hands trembled as she realized what it was—the journal her mother had given her when she was a child, the very same journal she had lost on a family vacation twenty years ago.

As she opened it, Joanna's breath caught in her throat. The pages were filled with handwriting, but not her own. It was her mother's. Tears welled in her eyes as she began to read the entries. Her mother, who had passed away years ago, had somehow received the journal after Joanna had lost it. The entries revealed a life Joanna had never known, a life where her mother had dedicated herself to research following her father's untimely death.

"I don't understand," Joanna whispered, her voice barely audible. "How did it end up here?"

Max suggested they run another test, hoping to reopen the portal and investigate further. Joanna hesitated, the weight of the unknown pressing heavily on her. But the chance to learn more about her mother's life was too compelling to ignore. She nodded, and they reactivated the machine.

The portal flickered to life once more, and this time, it remained stable. Joanna took a deep breath and stepped through, finding herself in her childhood home. The familiar scent of her mother's cooking and the sound of her father's laughter filled the air, pulling at her heartstrings. She saw her younger self asleep in her bed, clutching the journal tightly, and her mother sitting in the hallway, reading a newspaper article about a groundbreaking scientist who had just passed away. Joanna recognized the name immediately; it was her father.

Summoning her courage, Joanna approached her mother

cautiously. "Mom," she said softly, her voice trembling with emotion.

Her mother looked up, her eyes widening in shock. "Who are you?" she asked, her voice wary.

"I'm from the future," Joanna explained. "I have a message for you."

Her mother listened, her skepticism melting away as Joanna shared the contents of the journal and the story of her father's untimely death. Tears filled both their eyes as Joanna handed her mother the journal, realizing the magnitude of her actions.

With a newfound resolve, her mother promised to take care of their family and dedicate her life to the research that would ultimately lead to Joanna's breakthrough. Joanna hugged her mother tightly, feeling a sense of closure she hadn't realized she needed. She then stepped back through the portal, returning to the present.

Back at the lab, Max noticed the changes immediately. The research facility was more advanced, the equipment state-of-the-art. The team had accomplished far more than they had before. It was clear that her mother's dedication to the project had accelerated their progress.

As Joanna sat down, she felt the shift in her own life as well. Her relationship with her family was stronger, her father's presence a cherished memory. He had lived long enough to see her succeed, to witness the fruits of their combined labor.

She knew she had made a difference. For the first time in her life, Joanna felt a sense of completeness, a wholeness that transcended time. She had bridged the past and the present, forging a future bright with promise and filled with the love and legacy of her parents.

Christ Is Risen!

Once upon a time, in a small village nestled in the heart of a vast and beautiful country, there lived a close-knit community of devout Orthodox Christians. Their lives were simple, rooted in hard work on their farms and caring for their families, but their faith was their foundation. They cherished their traditions and beliefs, finding strength and unity in their shared spirituality.

One of the most significant traditions was the celebration of Eastern Orthodox Easter. This joyous occasion brought the entire village together to commemorate the resurrection of Jesus Christ and the triumph of life over death.

Weeks before Easter, the village buzzed with anticipation. Women gathered in kitchens, baking sweet bread, painting eggs in vibrant colors, and preparing traditional dishes for the feast. The aroma of freshly baked bread and spiced meats filled the air. Men spent long hours in the church, fasting, praying, and confessing their sins, seeking to purify their souls. Children, full of excitement, helped with the preparations, eager to play their part in the grand festivities.

On Holy Thursday, the village congregated in the church for

the solemn Service of the Twelve Gospels. The priest's voice resonated through the hallowed space as he read the Passion of Christ. The faithful listened in reverent awe, reliving the story of sacrifice and resurrection that lay at the heart of their faith.

Good Friday was a day of fasting and mourning. The villagers gathered to remember Jesus' death on the cross. They sang hymns and listened to the story of the Crucifixion. A somber procession circled the church, candles flickering in the twilight, as they carried icons and symbols of their journey with Jesus to the cross. Even in their mourning, they felt the approaching joy of the resurrection.

Saturday evening marked the Great Vigil of Easter. The village church was filled with anticipation and light as candles were lit, illuminating the faces of the faithful. Joyful Paschal hymns echoed through the night, and the priest's declaration, "Christ is risen!" was met with resounding cheers. The joyous feast of Easter began, spilling from homes into the streets. Families and friends shared food, drinks, stories, laughter, and song, celebrating late into the night.

For the next forty days, the village continued to celebrate the resurrection of Christ with a special liturgy each Sunday. They fasted and prayed, asking for the blessings of the Holy Spirit and preparing themselves for the coming of Pentecost.

As years passed, the village evolved, growing and changing with time. Yet, the tradition of Eastern Orthodox Easter remained a steadfast beacon of faith and community. Each year, the people gathered to celebrate the resurrection of their Lord, their faith growing stronger with each passing year.

In this small village, nestled in the heart of a vast and beautiful country, the celebration of Eastern Orthodox Easter was more than a holiday—it was a way of life. It symbolized the triumph of love over death and served as a poignant reminder of the sacrifice and resurrection of their Lord.

For the Orthodox Christians of that village, and for Orthodox Christians all over the world, Easter embodied a living testament to their faith. It was a celebration of enduring love and devotion, a renewal of their commitment to the teachings of Jesus Christ, and a joyous affirmation of their spiritual journey. And so, with unwavering faith and boundless joy, they proclaimed, "Christ is risen!" and their love for Jesus Christ continued to flourish and grow.

Spring Break Adventure

The sun shone brightly, casting its warm rays over the bustling city as Ava navigated the crowded streets towards the train station. Her long-awaited spring break trip was finally here, and she was beyond excited. After months of hard work and routine, she craved a break to explore new horizons and embrace adventure.

Settling into her seat on the train, Ava couldn't help but smile at the thought of the adventures awaiting her. The scenery outside the window was breathtaking, with rolling hills and lush green forests stretching as far as the eye could see. It felt like the beginning of a journey into a fairy-tale world, and she eagerly anticipated immersing herself in nature's beauty.

Several hours later, the train arrived at her destination—a quaint little town nestled amidst rolling hills and sprawling vineyards. Ava was immediately charmed by the place, with its narrow cobbled streets, brightly colored buildings, and the sweet aroma of blooming flowers filling the air.

She checked into a cozy bed and breakfast surrounded by a lush garden in full bloom. As she explored her surroundings, Ava was in awe of the vibrant life around her. The town bustled with locals going about their daily routines and tourists wandering the streets, soaking in the sights and sounds.

The next few days were filled with adventure. Ava explored the nearby countryside, visiting charming villages, sampling local cuisine, and taking in the stunning views from hilltop vantage points. Each morning, she rose early, eager to seize the day, and each evening she retired to bed, exhausted but content.

One morning, Ava decided to take a hot air balloon ride over the vineyards. As she soared above the rolling hills, she felt a profound sense of awe and wonder at the majesty of the landscape below. The sun was just beginning to rise, casting a golden glow over the fields, and the cool breeze was refreshing against her face.

The rest of the week brought more adventures. She went horseback riding through the countryside, visited a local farmers market brimming with fresh produce and handmade goods, and hiked through scenic mountain trails. Ava felt in her element, surrounded by the beauty of nature and the freedom of solo exploration.

As her trip neared its end, Ava realized that this spring break had been more than just a holiday; it had been a journey of self-discovery and growth. She returned home feeling refreshed and reinvigorated, ready to tackle whatever the future had in store.

The memories of her spring break adventure stayed with her,

a turning point in her life. She was grateful for the chance to escape the daily grind and immerse herself in nature's beauty. The charming little town, with its rolling hills and sprawling vineyards, held a special place in her heart. Ava knew she would always cherish the memories of her time there and the sense of renewal it had brought to her life.

Echoes of Eternity

In the heart of a bustling metropolis, amidst the towering skyscrapers and bustling streets, there lived a young artist named Maya. She had always felt a deep connection to the rhythms of the city—the pulse of life that echoed through its concrete veins. Yet, within her, there was a yearning for something beyond the urban chaos, something that whispered of ancient mysteries and timeless truths.

Maya spent her days working as a graphic designer in a sleek office building downtown. Her evenings were consumed by her true passion—painting. In the quiet solitude of her studio apartment, she would lose herself in swirls of color, creating canvases that captured glimpses of her inner world.

One rainy evening, as Maya sat by her window, sketching the silhouette of the city against the twilight sky, she heard a faint, haunting melody drifting through the raindrops. Intrigued, she followed the sound to an old bookstore tucked away in a forgotten corner of the city.

The bookstore, with its shelves overflowing with weathered volumes and the scent of aging paper, seemed to hold secrets of its own. As Maya wandered through the aisles, she stumbled upon a dusty leather-bound journal hidden behind a row of tattered classics. Curiosity piqued, she opened it and began to read.

The journal belonged to an artist from a bygone era—a kindred spirit who had once roamed the same streets and sought inspiration in the city's hidden corners. His words spoke of dreams and aspirations, of love lost and found, of the relentless pursuit of beauty in a world that often seemed indifferent.

Captivated by the artist's journey, Maya returned to the bookstore night after night, losing herself in the tales of forgotten romances and whispered legends. With each turn of the page, she felt herself drawn deeper into a realm where time seemed to stand still—a realm where echoes of eternity whispered through the pages of history.

Inspired by the artist's legacy, Maya poured her soul into her paintings, infusing each brushstroke with the essence of her newfound muse. Her artwork began to attract attention, drawing admirers from the art world and beyond. Yet, amidst the accolades and exhibitions, Maya remained haunted by the mystery of the journal and the enigmatic artist who had penned its pages.

One stormy night, as Maya retraced her steps to the bookstore, she discovered a hidden alcove behind a bookshelf—a place she had never noticed before. Inside, illuminated by flickering candlelight, was a collection of sketches and paintings—masterpieces that bore the unmistakable mark of the artist from the journal.

In that moment, Maya felt a profound connection to the past and the present—a realization that her own artistic journey was intertwined with those who had come before her. With reverence, she studied each painting, feeling as though she had uncovered a piece of her own soul reflected in the strokes of a brush.

As dawn broke over the city, Maya emerged from the bookstore with a sense of clarity and purpose. She knew now that her art was more than mere expression—it was a bridge between worlds, a testament to the enduring power of creativity and the timeless quest for meaning.

Years later, Maya's paintings adorned the walls of galleries around the world, each canvas a tribute to the echoes of eternity that had guided her path. Yet, amidst the acclaim and recognition, she never forgot the humble bookstore and the artist who had sparked her journey—a journey that had begun with a haunting melody and ended with a symphony of colors that echoed through the ages.

Resilience in Ink

In a quiet corner of the city, nestled between the towering buildings and bustling streets, there lived a writer named Emma. Her days were spent in the solitude of a small apartment, surrounded by stacks of notebooks filled with stories waiting to be told. For years, Emma had dreamed of seeing her words in print, of sharing her stories with the world.

But the road to publication had been paved with rejection slips and dashed hopes. Countless times, Emma had poured her heart into manuscripts only to receive polite rejections from publishers and agents alike. Each rejection felt like a blow, testing her resolve and shaking her belief in herself as a writer.

Yet, despite the setbacks, Emma refused to give up on her dreams. She found solace in the rhythmic tap-tap-tap of her keyboard late into the night, weaving tales of resilience and hope. Her characters became her companions, their journeys mirroring her own quest for validation and recognition.

One rainy afternoon, as Emma sat at her desk revising yet another manuscript, a letter arrived—an envelope that bore the familiar insignia of a publishing house she had long admired.

With trembling hands, she tore it open and read the words that would change her life.

"We are pleased to inform you…"

Tears of joy streamed down Emma's cheeks as she realized that her perseverance had paid off. Her novel had found a home, and soon, her words would be bound in ink and paper, ready to be shared with readers around the world.

The journey from rejection to acceptance had been arduous, filled with moments of doubt and despair. But through it all, Emma had discovered a strength within herself—a resilience that had carried her through the darkest days of uncertainty.

As she held her published book in her hands for the first time, Emma reflected on the lessons she had learned along the way. Rejection had taught her humility and perseverance. It had fueled her determination to hone her craft and sharpen her storytelling skills.

And as she embarked on book signings and readings, sharing her journey with aspiring writers and avid readers alike, Emma knew that her story was not just about success—it was about resilience in the face of adversity, about rising from rejection and embracing the possibilities that lay ahead.

In the quiet corner of the city where Emma had once toiled in anonymity, her name now adorned bookshelves and bestseller lists. But more importantly, her journey had become a beacon of hope for anyone who dared to dream, reminding them that every rejection is a stepping stone on the path to success.

For Emma, the writer who refused to give up, every rejection letter was now a testament to the strength of her spirit and the power of perseverance. And as she continued to write, her words echoed through the hearts of those who believed that dreams, no matter how daunting, were always worth pursuing.

* 9 7 9 8 2 2 7 4 6 8 7 5 8 *